DEDICATED TO

THIS BOOK IS DEDICATED TO ANY GRANNY THAT HAD TO STEP IN DUE TO CIRCUMSTANCES AN RAISE THEIR CHILDREN'S CHILDREN. THANK YOU FOR ALL YOU HAVE DONE, DOING, AND WILL DO!

THIS MORNING I GOT OUT OF BED.

ALL THE THINGS MY GRANNY SAID WERE STUCK IN MY HEAD.

YOU ARE SMART.

YOU ARE STRONG.

YOU ARE ONE OF A KIND.

IF YOU SEE IT.

YOU CAN BE IT.

IT'S ALL IN YOUR MIND.

SAY THIS WHEN YOU WAKE UP.

SAY THIS IN THE DAY.

SAY THIS BEFORE BED.

THIS IS WHAT GRANNY WOULD SAY!

GRANNY SAID, "CHILD, BE THANKFUL YOU LIVED ANOTHER DAY.

PUT BOTH HANDS IN THE AIR AND SHOUT. HURRAY!"

GRANNY SAID, "BRUSH YOUR TEETH AND WASH YOUR FACE.

HONEY, TAKE YOUR TIME. IT'S NOT A RACE."

GRANNY SAID, "CLEAN YOUR ROOM AND DO YOUR CHORES.

MAKE YOUR BED AND SWEEP THE FLOOR."

Granny said, "Monte, chew your food with your mouth closed."

SHE SAID, "FINISH YOUR BREAKFAST

AND PUT ON YOUR SCHOOL CLOTHES."

Granny said, "Tuck in your shirt and wear matching socks."

She said, "Don't forget your homework or your lunchbox."

GRANNY SAID, "LOOK BOTH WAYS BEFORE YOU CROSS THE STREET.

BE NICE TO YOUR TEACHER AND ALL THE KIDS YOU MEET."

Then Granny gave me a big hug to start my day.

She said, "Honey, say with me every word that I say."

SCHOOL

YOU ARE SMART.

YOU ARE STRONG.

YOU ARE ONE OF A KIND.

IF YOU SEE IT.

YOU CAN BE IT.

IT'S ALL IN YOUR MIND.

SAY THIS when you wake up.

SAY THIS in the day.

SAY THIS BEFORE BED.

THIS IS WHAT GRANNY WOULD SAY!

I could still hear her voice as I sat at my desk.

Granny would say, "Monte, do your best."

I'm
Smart

Granny said, "Be respectful.

Use the golden rule.

Treat others the way you want them to treat you."

Thank you.

GRANNY SAID, "BE TRUSTWORTHY.

DO WHAT YOU SAY YOU WILL DO.

DO THE RIGHT THING EVEN IF THE ONLY ONE DOING THE RIGHT THING IS YOU."

Granny said, "Honey, be fair. Take turns and share.

Help people in need. Show you care."

GRANNY SAID, "BABY, BE RESPONSIBLE.

THINK BEFORE YOU DO. THERE MAY BE SOMEONE SMALLER WHO LOOKS UP TO YOU."

NEWS

GRANNY SAID, "BE A GOOD CITIZEN. OBEY ALL THE RULES.

MAKE YOUR SCHOOL A BETTER PLACE FOR OTHERS AND FOR YOU."

_ Classroom Rules
_Respect the speaker.
_follow instructions the first
they are given.
_Be respectful of your peers.

When I got home, Granny asked, "Monte, how was your day?

Honey, say with me every word that I say."

You are smart.

You are strong.

You are one of a kind.

If you see it.

You can be it.

It's all in your mind.

SAY THIS WHEN YOU WAKE UP.

SAY THIS IN THE DAY.

SAY THIS BEFORE BED.

THIS IS WHAT GRANNY WOULD SAY!

I can still hear all my Granny's words in my ear.

I smile and say to myself, "I wish she was still here."

End

About the Author

Lamont Pretrell Muhammed is an author, teacher, hip hop artist and public speaker. He currently serves his community of Waterloo, Iowa by using his gifts and talents to mentor, educate, motivate and elevate human potential.

For more information and services, contact Mr. Muhammed at:

theiamprogram@gmail.com

Made in the USA
Monee, IL
26 July 2020

37025927R00031